First to Fly

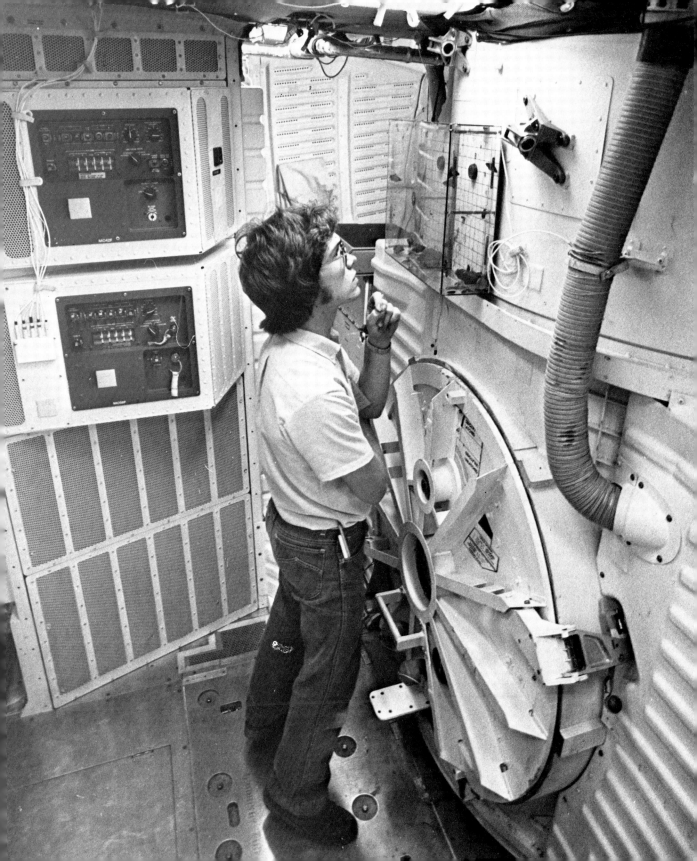

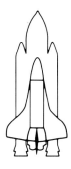

First to Fly

Robert R. Moulton

Foreword by
Lt. Gen. James A. Abrahamson

Lerner Publications Company   **Minneapolis**

Page 2: Todd Nelson and his insect experiment in the space shuttle mock-up at Johnson Space Center, Houston, Texas

Library of Congress Cataloging in Publication Data

Moulton, Robert R.
    First to fly.

    Summary: An account of eighteen-year-old Todd Nelson's experiment, "Insect in Flight Motion Study," which was the first student experiment ever to fly aboard a manned space shuttle flight.
    1. Insects—Flight. 2. Space biology. 3. Space shuttles. [1. Insects—Flight. 2. Space biology. 3. Experiments] I. Title.
QL496.7.M68   1983   595.7'01'852   83-11971
ISBN 0-8225-1576-8 (lib. bdg.)

Manufactured in the United States of America

1 2 3 4 5 6 7 8 9 10 92 91 90 89 88 87 86 85 84 83

For my daughter, Tara, and my son, Collin,
Pathfinders in their own right

CONTENTS

FOREWORD

Much has been said recently about the decline of science education in the United States and of our ability to develop students with the necessary skills to compete in an increasingly technological world. Throughout all levels of government, in school systems, in educational associations, and in private industry, this concern is being addressed, and it has resulted in a commitment to achieve new levels of excellence.

As its contribution to stimulate the study and teaching of science in the nation's secondary schools, the National Aeronautics and Space Administration has established the Shuttle Student Involvement Project (SSIP). This annual competition invites high school students to propose experiments suitable for flight aboard the Space Shuttle. The competition phase of the project is administered for NASA by the National Science Teachers Association, one of the leaders in the current movement to revitalize science education.

The SSIP program also receives the enthusiastic support and cooperation of many U.S. industries and universities. These institutions commit resources and guidance by becoming sponsors of those students who emerge through the rigorous competition process to become national winners. It is through this phase of the program that the students turn their winning proposals into flight-ready experiments.

In *First to Fly,* Bob Moulton offers a behind-the-scenes look at the SSIP process and how one sponsor, Honeywell, Inc., helped prepare a student experiment, Todd Nelson's "Insect in Flight Motion Study," for the third mission of the Space Shuttle *Columbia.* The efforts of this research team helped to pave the way and define the procedures for student experiments to be flown on future Shuttle missions. *First to Fly* is not only a story about one student's experience in completing an experiment, but it can also serve as a guide for those students and teachers who intend to participate in upcoming SSIP competitions.

In my judgment, the Space Shuttle has launched a new revolution in space exploration. With every flight, we take another step toward the establishment of a routine operational system that will open the environment of space to new discoveries, new developments, and new products. We feel it happening. The Shuttle Student Involvement Project and the students, teachers, and sponsors who have participated in all aspects of the program are making an important contribution to this revolution.

Just as the Shuttle was conceived and developed by visionary leaders and dreamers from the pioneering days of the space program, I believe that among today's student population are the leaders and dreamers for our next step in space. Perhaps these new leaders will be motivated by their participation in programs like SSIP, which first gave them the opportunity to touch their dreams. I look forward with great confidence and expectation to the achievements that they will create.

LIEUTENANT GENERAL JAMES A. ABRAHAMSON
Associate Administrator for Space Flight
National Aeronautics and Space Administration

First to Fly

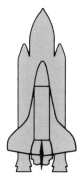

Introduction

It was 11 P.M. on the night of March 21, 1982. The weather at Cape Canaveral's Kennedy Space Center in Florida was calm and warm. The sky was filled with stars. Todd Nelson, an 18-year-old high school student from Rose Creek, Minnesota, stood alone enjoying the quiet of the warm Florida night. There was nothing he could do now but wait.

It had been more than a year since Todd had written his proposal for a science experiment to be conducted on the space shuttle *Columbia*. Now, after eight months of hard work—of trial and error, success and failure, design and redesign —Todd's "bug" experiment was stowed aboard *Columbia*, scheduled to go into space at 10 A.M. the next morning.

Lit by powerful floodlights, the space shuttle *Columbia* **waits on the launch pad for its journey into space.**

The shuttle's rocket engines
ignite in a burst of flame.

Looking out toward the launch pad, Todd could see *Columbia* standing majestically, lit by bright floodlights. The powerful lights bounced off the white body of the shuttle, creating a filmy glow around it. With its giant fuel tank and two booster rockets, *Columbia* looked like a magic castle that would not be out of place at Disney World, located a few miles away.

Around 5 A.M., dawn washed the sky with pale reds and oranges. The launch clock was already running, counting down the hours and minutes until 10 o'clock. Then a technical problem forced an hour-long delay, and launch was reset for 11 A.M.

At 11 A.M. Eastern Standard Time, it was finally "GO"! The earth started to tremble under Todd's feet as the biggest rocket package ever used to launch a space vehicle ignited, began to burn, then thundered to full power. *Columbia* stood for a moment on a tail of red and yellow fire and then moved slowly upward, the burning rocket fuel bellowing and crackling. The shuttle tore through the low-hanging clouds and reappeared

Todd Nelson (right) and his parents watch *Columbia's* **ascent.**

above them in the blue morning sky, its tail of fire visible thousands of feet overhead. Todd and his parents, Dale and Sherry, craned their necks to watch *Columbia* soar out of sight.

In the middeck of the space shuttle, tucked neatly away in a locker drawer below pilot Gordon Fullerton, was Todd's "Insect in Flight Motion Study" experiment, the first student experiment ever to fly aboard a manned shuttle flight.

Enter...
Your experiment in space

NSTA-NASA SPACE SHUTTLE STUDENT INVOLVEMENT PROGRAM

The National Science Teachers Association and the National Aeronautics and Space Administration are offering to students the unique opportunity to propose space experiments to be performed aboard the Space Shuttle.

ELIGIBILITY:
Any student in U.S. public, private, parochial, or U.S. overseas schools in grades 9-12.

TO ENTER:
Ask your teacher to request an official entry form, rules booklet, and Space Shuttle Student Experiment Guide from:

SPACE SHUTTLE PROGRAM
National Science Teachers Association
1742 Connecticut Avenue, N.W.
Washington, D.C. 20009

Prepare a proposal, not to exceed 1,000 words, describing your proposed space experiment in accordance with the Space Shuttle Project Rules Booklet.

DEADLINE:
Proposals must be received by your NSTA Regional Director no later than February 2, 1981.

AWARDS:
Certificates of participation will be awarded to all entrants.

REGIONAL WINNERS:
The 20 best proposals in each region will be selected as regional winners by local committees. Regional winners and their teacher/advisors will participate, with expenses paid, in the Space Shuttle symposium to be held in each region, where ideas will be shared with other winners and experts in aerospace science and technology. Certificates will be awarded to regional winners, their teacher/advisors and to their schools.

NATIONAL WINNERS:
All regional winning proposals will be evaluated by a national committee and 10 finalists will be selected from these as national winners. The 10 national winners and their teacher/advisors will be invited to attend, with expenses paid, the Space Shuttle symposium at the Kennedy Space Center. At this program there will be presentation of awards and further discussion of the nature and conduct of science in space. The winners and their teacher/advisors and their schools will receive special medallions. All national winners will be considered by NASA for possible flight on a future Space Shuttle mission.

NATIONAL SCIENCE TEACHERS ASSOCIATION
1742 CONNECTICUT AVENUE, N.W., WASHINGTON, D.C. 20009

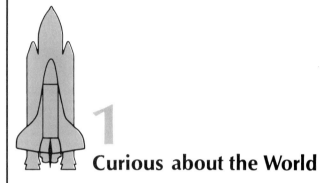

1 Curious about the World

Todd Nelson first learned about the Shuttle Student Involvement Project (SSIP) in the fall of 1980, when he was a junior at Southland High School in Adams, Minnesota, located about 15 miles from his home in Rose Creek. He saw a poster in his science classroom inviting students to enter the first annual SSIP competition, which was sponsored jointly by the National Aeronautics and Space Administration (NASA) and the National Science Teachers Association (NSTA). The winners of the competition would receive a very special prize: they would be given a chance to have their scientific experiments conducted by astronauts on board the space shuttle.

The poster announcing the Shuttle Student Involvement Project competition

The posters on the wall in Todd's room reflect his interest in the space program.

Bob Roberts, Todd's science teacher, encouraged Todd to develop an experiment that could be entered in this unusual competition. He knew that Todd had a keen interest in the space program and a good general background in science. In his physics, chemistry, and biology courses, Todd had learned about experimentation and the scientific method of investigation. Todd was a creative, enthusiastic student, and Bob Roberts was sure

20

that he could come up with a proposal for a practical experiment that could be conducted in the weightlessness of space.

Like all scientists, Todd drew the ideas for his experiment from his observations of the world around him. In the fields and woods of his family's small farm, he had many opportunities to observe the wonders of the natural world. One of the things he was most interested in was the phenomenon of flight—the ways in which many living creatures were able to defy the force of gravity and move freely through the air.

On warm summer days, Todd watched dragonflies hover near him like helicopters. Their large, translucent wings held their slender bodies in flight while they seemed to return his stare with their bulging eyes. He admired the swooping grace of the barn swallows as they dove at near supersonic speeds to snatch insects out of the air. Todd noticed how different their flight was from that of the bulky pigeons, which flapped wide wings against the wind and landed clumsily to strut around on the ground, pecking at tiny insects.

On rainy days, Todd found things to do in his room, building model airplanes or molding ceramic shapes to be fired in the kiln at school. While he worked, he couldn't avoid the pesky houseflies that buzzed and zoomed around his head. He knew that flies have tiny balancing organs called "halteres" behind their wings to help them retain stability in flight. If its halteres were removed, a fly couldn't control its flight. It would zig and zag erratically or wouldn't fly at all.

Working with ceramics is one of Todd's hobbies.

When the long summer days were over on the Nelson farm, darkness brought moths that beat their dusty wings against the light on the front porch. If a moth managed to get inside the house, it went immediately to a lamp, circling wildly and smacking against the shade again and again. Todd wondered why moths were attracted to light and how their flight was affected by it.

Todd's closest association with the insect world was with the honeybees that he kept in wooden hives behind his house. He raised the bees for the honey they produced, and as he cared for them, he observed their habits. He watched their reactions to the world around them—to rain, cold, sun, and to the beekeeper himself. He saw and heard their rapid wingbeats.

In studying honeybees, Todd learned that the insects use the light of the sun to guide their flight when they leave the hive in search of food. Thanks to their efficient navigation system, the bees could return to the hive loaded down with the nectar that would be transformed into sweet golden honey. Todd knew that when his bees flew from flower to flower gathering nectar, they were also carrying pollen that fertilized the plants and allowed them to reproduce.

Todd was fascinated by the way his honeybees navigated in flight and by all the other examples of flight dynamics that he saw around him. He did not limit his interest only to observations, however. One of his favorite pastimes during the summer was flying model gliders that he built himself. In order to build and fly these graceful

Todd's interest in insects began at an early age. In this childhood photograph, Todd is posing with a monarch butterfly.

planes, Todd had to understand the principles that allowed a glider to soar through the air without power after it was launched.

Soaring gliders, hovering dragonflies, moths that circled madly around a light—flight in all its forms aroused Todd's curiosity. When he found out about the SSIP competition, Todd realized that he had a unique opportunity to look for answers to some of his questions. Flying creatures on earth had to deal with the force of gravity, but what would happen if the same creatures tried to fly in the zero gravity of space? How would insects navigate in a weightless environment? Would their flight control systems function in the same way that they did on earth? Could honeybees fly well enough under weightless conditions to pollinate plants in a space colony?

One of Todd's model planes

These were some of the questions that were in Todd Nelson's mind when he began planning his experiment for the SSIP competition. Like other scientific experiments, Todd's "Insect in Flight Motion Study" was inspired by curiosity about the natural world and a desire to understand how it works.

As an amateur beekeeper, Todd learned a lot about the habits of insects.

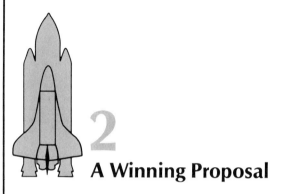

2
A Winning Proposal

Science competition was not new to Todd. Just the year before, he had designed and built a model of a hovercraft that had won a special award from the United States Navy in a Science Fair competition. But the Shuttle Student Involvement Project was different. For this competition Todd had to write a formal proposal for "a project to be done, experiment, demonstration or activities to be performed by astronauts in a Space Shuttle mission." Todd's proposal would be judged on the basis of clarity, organization, and, most important, scientific validity. It would have to meet the same kind of standards as an experiment planned by a professional scientist.

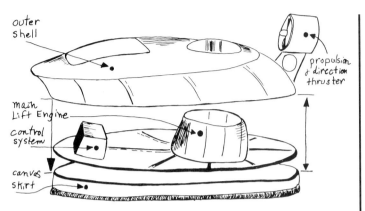

outer shell

propulsion & direction thruster

main lift engine

control system

canvas skirt

Todd's model of a hovercraft won a special award in a Science Fair competition.

Before Todd wrote his proposal, he sat down to talk with his science teacher, Bob Roberts. Bob had helped him with other science competitions, and Todd was eager to have his teacher's advice. He told Bob about his idea for an experiment that would test flight dynamics in space. "The shuttle project would be a great chance to see how earth insects fly in zero gravity," he said.

Bob Roberts agreed. "You could put insects on the space shuttle in some kind of container and study their reactions to weightlessness."

"Weightlessness would be the variable in my experiment, right? The one thing that would be different from the insects' normal environment?"

"That's right," Bob answered. "You'd be comparing the insects' flight in zero gravity with their normal flight on earth."

Todd thought for a minute. "Well," he said, "from what I know about the mechanics of flight, I bet that earth insects will have trouble flying in zero gravity. That would be my hypothesis—the idea that I'd be testing in my experiment."

"That's a good place to start," Bob Roberts said, "but a scientific hypothesis has to be a little more specific than that. Why don't you work on a first draft of your proposal and I'll review it with you."

A few days later, Todd brought in a draft of his proposal for an "Insect in Flight Motion Study." When Bob Roberts looked it over, he was pleased with what his student had accomplished.

Todd had begun his proposal by pointing out how important gravity seems to be in normal insect flight on earth. "In a way, insect flight mechanisms are really adaptations to overcome gravity. . . . A large amount of insect flight energy is used to provide lift." Because of this, Todd suggested, "it would be of value to observe flight behavior adjustment in the absence of gravity." Then Todd presented his hypothesis: "In the absence of gravity . . . , insects should encounter orientation and flight adjustment problems, depending upon their mass-to-wing ratios."

Following Bob Robert's advice, Todd had made his hypothesis more specific by suggesting that the insects' flight problems might be affected by the difference between the size of their wings and the size of their bodies. It was this idea—this theory—about insect flight that Todd's experiment would test.

In writing his proposal for the SSIP competition, Todd relied on the advice of his science teacher, Bob Roberts (left).

In developing an hypothesis and planning an experiment to test it, Todd was following a procedure used by scientists all over the world. This same method of thought is also used in a more informal way by many people who have never been inside a laboratory. A man who wakes up one morning with a headache, a fever, and sore muscles thinks, "It's probably the flu. There's a lot of it around." This person has an hypothesis about his condition that can be tested by going to the doctor. A mechanic who hears a strange clanking noise in a car engine might come up with the hypothesis that something is wrong with the carburetor. In order to test the hypothesis, the mechanic examines the engine. If the carburetor is fine, then it's time to come up with another theory to explain the engine's problem.

A scientist usually tests an hypothesis by a careful method of experimentation. Todd Nelson understood how that method worked, and he described it in his SSIP proposal:

> The experiment to test the hypothesis will be performed on earth and in space. Both control and experimental tests will be performed under uniform temperature, pressure, and light conditions. The experimental variable will be the absence of gravity in space flight.

By comparing the flight behavior of a control group of insects observed in the normal gravity of earth to the behavior of insects in space, Todd could give his hypothesis a good test. All conditions would be the same in each location except for the one variable, the absence of gravity in space. If the space insects had more trouble flying than those on earth, then weightlessness would be the most likely cause and Todd's hypothesis would be confirmed.

As test subjects, Todd chose some of the insects he had observed in flight: the monarch butterfly, the bumblebee, the common housefly, and the dragonfly. He picked the bumblebee and monarch butterfly because they were direct opposites in the ratios between the size of their wings and their bodies. The butterfly had large wings in relation to its body mass, while the bumblebee's wings were small compared to its large body. Todd

Top to bottom: The monarch butterfly, the bumblebee, the housefly, and the dragonfly.

wanted to test his favorite, the honeybee, but he and Bob Roberts decided that the bumblebee was a better subject for this kind of comparison.

The housefly and the dragonfly didn't have such extreme differences in size of wings and bodies, but they did have other features that made them worth including in an experiment on flight. Todd chose the common housefly because of its tiny gyroscopes, or halteres, used for in-flight stabilization. He planned to include some flies with their halteres removed in order to see how their flight control was affected. Finally, Todd proposed that dragonflies be used "to observe [their] unique flight behavior similar to helicopter hovering."

Todd's proposal included not only a list of the insect subjects for the experiment but also a description of the container that would hold them. As Todd explained, "The test chamber should contain adequate volume necessary for insect flight, allow for safe handling of insects, and confine them to a chamber."

It would not be easy to design a container that satisfied all these requirements, yet was small enough to fit into a stowage locker on the shuttle that was not much bigger than a desk drawer. Todd tried to solve this problem by proposing that the walls of the container be made of a flexible material. This would make it possible to collapse the flight chamber like a tent for storage in the small locker and to expand it during the actual test so that the insects would have room to fly. Todd included drawings and diagrams of this collapsible flight chamber in his proposal.

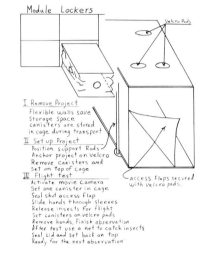

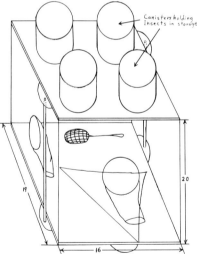

Todd's plans for a collapsible flight chamber

One of the most important parts of any experiment is recording the results, and Todd had given serious thought to this requirement. His proposal included a section on "data collection," which presented his ideas on the subject:

The nature of the experiment requires a visual approach to data collection. A movie camera will be used to record the entire flight performance, collision with the walls of the test chamber, coordination, directional orientation, and maneuverability of each insect for later interpretation. A high speed movie camera will be necessary to record wing beats per second, possibly showing new adaptations in wing beat patterns, aiding in flight. . . .

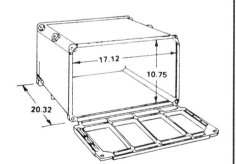

The flight chamber had to fit into a small locker drawer (above) located in the middeck of the shuttle (right).

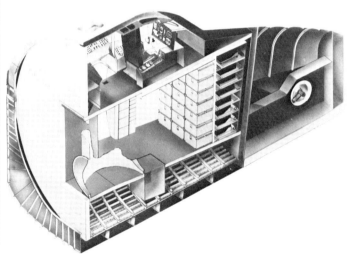

All data will be used to establish comparison relationships among the insects tested to find whether certain species are more adapted for space flight.

Todd concluded his SSIP proposal with these words: "The results from the insect in flight motion observation will . . . answer old questions and will also raise new questions about the nature of flight in absence of gravity."

Going over Todd's proposal carefully, Bob Roberts was happy to see that his student had made a real effort to use the methods of scientific investigation that he had learned in his science classes. Bob helped to put the finishing touches on the proposal, and then Todd typed the final draft, finishing it just in time to make the February 1, 1981 deadline.

A couple of weeks later, Todd and Bob Roberts got the good news that Todd's proposal had been selected as one of 20 regional winners in the SSIP competition. Both student and teacher were invited to attend a conference at NASA's Lewis Research Center in Cleveland, Ohio, along with the 19 other winners in their region.

This regional meeting was a very special part of the Shuttle Student Involvement Project. It provided an opportunity for each of the 20 winners to present his or her proposal and to discuss it with the other students. No judging would be done on the regional level, and at the end of the conference, all 20 students would submit their proposals in the final stage of the competition.

The teachers attending the Cleveland meeting were impressed with its results. Bob Roberts said, "It was really great! A very good demonstration of science at work. All those young scientists working together, making suggestions, helping each other improve the design of their experiments, just as professional scientists do."

Todd's reaction was also positive. "I enjoyed it because there was no competition between us, just helping each other out. That's really different from the Science Fairs. It helped make my experiment better."

After the regional meeting, the student winners

The regional winners of the SSIP competition at the meeting held in Cleveland, Ohio. Todd is in the bottom row, third from the right.

```
☐ ☑        ⌴ ⌴      ☐ ☐     ☐ ☐ ☐ ☐
Region     State   Grade   Serial No.    Topic _____
                            (OFFICE USE ONLY)

             SPACE SHUTTLE STUDENT INVOLVEMENT PROJECT

                  STUDENT ENTRY FORM - REGION VII

     STUDENT:  Fill out this form completely (TYPE OR PRINT).)  Ask your
Teacher-Advisor to read your proposal and sign this form.  Then staple
this completed entry form to the front of your proposal.  Send it to the
Regional Director, Mr. LeRoy Lee, Wisconsin Junior Academy, 1922 University
Avenue, Madison, WI. 53705.  DO NOT SEND REPORTS TO NASA OR NSTA.  Signing
this entry form indicates your understanding and acceptance of the official
rules.  All entries must be received no later than February 2, 1981.  USE
FIRST CLASS MAIL.  (Please enclose a stamped, self-addressed postal card
so we can acknowledge receipt of your entry.)  ALL proposals become the
property of NASA.

     1.  STUDENT NAME  Todd          E        Nelson
                      (first)    (Initial)    (last)

         HOME ADDRESS   RR # 1 Box 73

         CITY AND STATE   Rose Creek, Minn          (zip code)  55970

         HOME PHONE NUMBER  507 433 4804            GRADE      11

     2.  SCHOOL NAME       Southland Public School

         SCHOOL ADDRESS _____(telephone)  507 582 3568

         CITY AND STATE     Adams, Minn.           (zip code)  55909

         PRINCIPAL'S NAME  Mr. Lawrence E. Croker

     3.  NAME OF TEACHER-ADVISOR  Robert      D       Roberts
                                 (first)  (initial)   (last)

         ADDRESS       Box 47

         CITY AND STATE  Elkton, Minn.              (zip code)  55933

     4.  TITLE OF PROPOSAL  Insect In Flight Motion Study

            SUBJECT AREA    Biological Science

                            SIGNATURES

I have read the rules and all of the information on the entry materials for
the Space Shuttle Student Involvement Project.  I certify that the attached
proposal is the student's own work.

     STUDENT SIGNATURE _____

     TEACHER-ADVISOR SIGNATURE _____

List ALL ACKNOWLEDGEMENTS (Rules Book, p. 7) on the back of this form only.
```

had two weeks to rewrite their experiments before submitting them to NSTA for final judging. Todd went back to Rose Creek and worked on his proposal, sharpening it and including some of the suggestions made by the other students at the regional meeting. After Todd and Bob Roberts reviewed the proposal one final time, they sent it off to NSTA headquarters in Washington, D.C. Then they sat back to wait for the judges' decision.

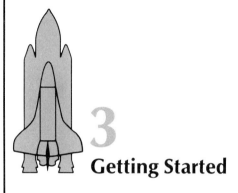

3
Getting Started

In May 1981, Dr. Glen Wilson of NASA and Dorothy Culbert of NSTA announced the winners of the first Shuttle Student Involvement Project from NASA headquarters in Washington, D.C. Todd Nelson of Rose Creek, Minnesota, and 9 other student scientists had won a chance to have an experiment performed in space aboard the space shuttle!

The next stage in the project would be a conference in August at Kennedy Space Center, where the 10 winners would be able to discuss their experiments with NASA scientists before beginning work on them. Also attending the meeting would be representatives of private companies and organizations that would act as sponsors for

The 10 national winners attended a conference at Kennedy Space Center in August 1981. Here they met with representatives of the corporations and institutions that would sponsor their experiments.

the student experiments. Some of the sponsors were contractors that manufactured the complex equipment used in the space program. Others, like the Explorers Club of New York City, were organizations that encouraged exploration of the natural world, on earth and in space. Among the many famous explorers who have been helped by the Explorers Club is Thor Heyerdahl, who in 1947 crossed the Pacific Ocean on the raft Kon Tiki to test his theory about the settlements of the Polynesian islands.

One of the corporations invited to sponsor an SSIP experiment was the Avionics Division of

Honeywell, Inc., supplier of flight systems on every U.S. manned space flight and of several key systems on the space shuttle. Honeywell, whose headquarters are located in Minneapolis, Minnesota, was pleased to see that a Minnesota student was among the 10 winners. The company chose Todd Nelson's "Insect in Flight Motion Study" as the experiment it would sponsor.

Dr. J. Robert Peterson was picked to head a team of Honeywell engineers and technicians who would help Todd get his experiment ready to fly. The team members would share with Todd the job of deciding exactly how the experiment would be performed, of designing and building the necessary equipment, of choosing the insect subjects. Like most scientific projects, Todd's experiment would be a cooperative venture, requiring the skills of many different people.

On his way to the student conference at Kennedy Space Center in August, Todd visited Dr. Bob Peterson at his Honeywell office in Clearwater, Florida. Peterson introduced Todd and his experiment to Stath Lenardos and Cliff Williams, program managers of the shuttle flight control system and main engine control system, both of which were manufactured by Honeywell. Peterson was as interested as Todd was in what the two space engineers would have to say about the "Insect in Flight Motion Study." Todd discussed his experiment with Lenardos and Williams, and at the end of the day, they gave their opinion. They thought that the experiment would work. Todd's proposal had passed its first review by space engineers.

Above: Bob Peterson (second from left) meets with Todd and space engineers Stath Lenardos (left) and Cliff Williams (center). Below: Stath Lenardos talks with Todd about the experiment proposal.

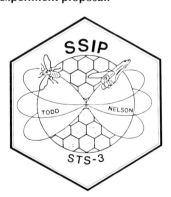

At a press conference held in Florida on August 26, 1981, Robert R. Moulton of Honeywell (below, right) introduced Todd and his experiment to the public.

When Todd visited the Honeywell Avionics facility in Minneapolis, he met Joy Mountford, a senior research scientist in the Systems and Research Center.

The first formal design review of Todd's experiment was held at this Honeywell plant in September.

Peterson scheduled the first formal "design review" of Todd's experiment for September 21 in Minneapolis, about a month after the student conference. This review would take Todd's proposal apart and put it back together again, making any changes that might improve its chances to fly on a manned space mission.

When Todd Nelson and Bob Roberts came to the Honeywell conference room on September 21, they were introduced to a whole crew of experts. Dr. Bob Peterson was there, along with fellow Honeywellers Walt Posingies, engineer; Bob Buda, engineer, amateur entomologist, and beekeeper;

Jerry Adams, design and engineering technician; Bill Steinbicker, professional photographer and manager of Honeywell video and film services; and Tom Jaglo, specialist in high-speed photography. Representing Honeywell as Todd's sponsor was Robert Moulton, the author of this book, whose job it was to coordinate the entire project.

After introductions were made, Todd outlined his proposal to the group, stating his hypothesis and showing his drawings of the flight chamber and his list of insect subjects. He also explained how he thought the astronauts would perform the experiment. Everyone knew that some changes would have to be made in the original proposal since Todd had written it without knowing how long the shuttle flight might be or how many astronauts would be available to conduct his experiment. At the SSIP conference in Florida, Todd and Bob Peterson had decided to shoot for STS-3, a seven-day mission scheduled for January 1982, with two astronauts on board. With this information, the real work could begin.

Todd's choice of insects was the first item to be discussed. Bob Buda was concerned about the lifespan of some of the insects. Would they live long enough for the STS-3 mission? "Remember, the insects would have to be in space for a week, and we don't know when during that week the crew would film them in flight." Bob also wondered about the compatibility of the "insectronauts." Stored in the shuttle locker, would they attack and eat each other before the experiment would even begin?

Engineer Bob Buda's experience as a beekeeper made him a valuable advisor for Todd's project.

Todd said, "Mr. Buda has a good point. We have to be sure that the insects we use have an adult lifespan of at least a week. And dragonflies could be a real problem if they weren't separated from the other insects as I suggested in my drawings. They're real predators."

Todd went on, "At the student conference in Florida, Bob Peterson and I talked about the possibility of changing the kind of insects we use to make the experiment simpler."

Peterson nodded. "I think that's the key," he said. "The more Todd can simplify the experiment, the better chance he has of getting it flown. Maybe he should even change his hypothesis so it's not a study of insects with different body and wing sizes."

"Mr. Peterson and I talked about using just two kinds of insects, houseflies and honeybees," Todd added. "If we did that, we could compare the flight control of the two insects—the flies with their halteres and the bees without."

Bob Buda said that in his opinion honeybees would be a better choice than the bumblebees originally proposed. "More is known about them," Buda said, "and that makes them better subjects for an experiment because you'll be able to compare what you see in weightlessness with what is already known about their flight behavior. But," he went on, "I wonder if honeybees will survive if they're taken out of the hive for such a long time. They're social insects, you know, and they always live in groups. You'll have to find out before you decide to use them."

    Steinbicker and Jaglo, the photography experts, went along with simplifying the experiment, but they had their own special concerns. Honeybees and houseflies might be too small to photograph successfully. "It would be easier to get good pictures of larger insects," Steinbicker said. "It's not impossible to film bees and flies, but Todd will have to be sure that the astronauts have the right camera lenses on board."

    Jaglo agreed, and so did Peterson and the other team members. What good was his experiment if Todd wasn't able to collect data that was good enough to support his hypothesis? He had to get good pictures.

The group went on to discuss the container in which Todd's insectronauts would ride. Jerry Adams, the design technician, had some questions about Todd's "bug box." "I think that the collapsible box Todd designed is good, but he should be sure that once it's out of the tray and expanded, it will stand up well enough for the crew to get good photographs. The box would be sturdier if the sides were rigid instead of flexible."

Steinbicker pointed out that rigid sides would also be better for filming. "I'm not sure that collapsible sides could be stretched tight enough to get good pictures. Any ridges or bumps in that flexible material and light will bounce off the container. That could ruin the photographs."

"I used the collapsible sides so I could get more insects in the box and have room for them to fly," Todd said. "If we use fewer and smaller insects, maybe we could use a box with rigid sides. I think that's a good idea."

Suggestions flew back and forth as the team members took Todd's experiment apart and put it back together, streamlining it, broadening it, and sometimes coming back to where Todd had started. Peterson and the other scientists had done this many times, and they were good at it. Bob Roberts beamed with pleasure. His student was seeing the scientific method at work firsthand and playing a part in it.

When the design review meeting was over, there were still decisions left to be made and plenty of work to be done. Jerry Adams' assignment was to make some sketches of a flight chamber with

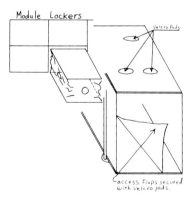

The experts believed that Todd's collapsible container might cause problems in filming the experiment.

rigid sides and discuss them with Todd. Bob Peterson said that he would get in touch with John Jackson, the NASA official responsible for integrating student experiments into the shuttle missions, and find out what kind of camera lenses would be available on *Columbia.* He would also let John know about the other things that had been discussed at the meeting.

Bob Peterson's other big job would be to set up a schedule for getting Todd's experiment ready to fly. "There are two major parts of the experiment that have to be outlined in the schedule," he said, "designing and building the flight chamber and making the final choice of insects. If we're going to make STS-3 in January, we really have to hustle!"

Todd was not very happy when he left that first design review meeting. "They tore my experiment apart," he said. "They tore it apart!"

Bob Roberts and Bob Peterson tried to explain. "Every experiment goes through the same thing, just like every engineering job we do," Peterson said. "Those men spent their entire day talking about your experiment. If they hadn't thought they could help you make it work, they wouldn't have been there."

Roberts added, "Todd, this is how scientists work. By talking about all the problems and the things that might go wrong, we'll be able to develop an experiment that will give your hypothesis a real test."

Bob Roberts smiled. Todd's education in science was just beginning.

John Jackson

A draft of the timetable for Todd's experiment

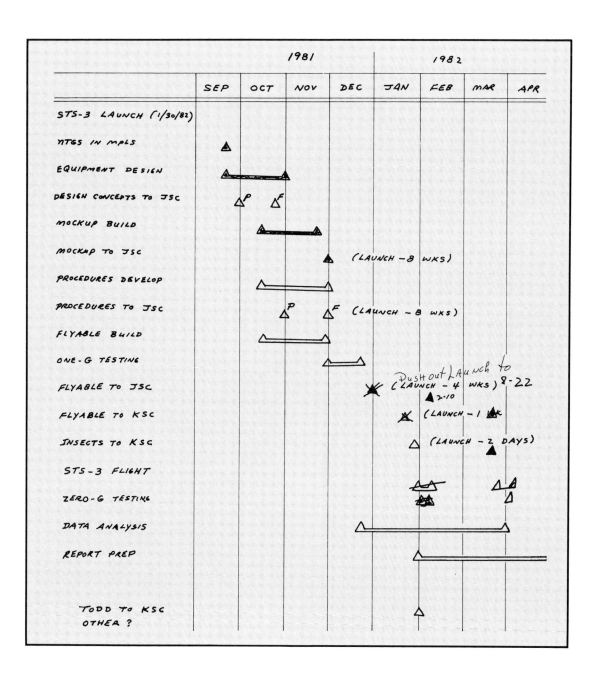

	1981				1982			
	SEP	OCT	NOV	DEC	JAN	FEB	MAR	APR
STS-3 LAUNCH (1/30/82)								
NTGS IN MPLS								
EQUIPMENT DESIGN								
DESIGN CONCEPTS TO JSC		P F						
MOCKUP BUILD								
MOCKUP TO JSC				(LAUNCH - 8 WKS)				
PROCEDURES DEVELOP								
PROCEDURES TO JSC			P	F (LAUNCH - 8 WKS)				
FLYABLE BUILD								
ONE-G TESTING								
FLYABLE TO JSC				(LAUNCH - 4 WKS)	Push out Launch to 8-22			
FLYABLE TO KSC					(LAUNCH - 1 WK) 2-10			
INSECTS TO KSC					(LAUNCH - 2 DAYS)			
STS-3 FLIGHT								
ZERO-G TESTING								
DATA ANALYSIS								
REPORT PREP								
TODD TO KSC OTHER ?								

47

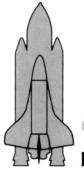

4 Building the Flight Chamber

Todd and Jerry Adams began work on the new design of the flight chamber immediately after the design review meeting in September. In planning this important part of Todd's experiment, they couldn't build on the work of other scientists, as would normally be done. No scientific experiment of this kind had ever been conducted before. To design a successful container, Todd and Jerry would have to do basic research, using the trial-and-error method. And they would have to do it under the pressure of a tight deadline. To make the third shuttle flight in January, they *had* to stick to the schedule Bob Peterson had drawn up.

Jerry and Todd's first design for the flight chamber was simple. It was for a rigid box small enough to fit into one of the shuttle locker drawers, which

Todd with a prototype of the flight chamber

measured 10 inches high, 17 inches wide, and 20 inches deep (25 centimeters high, 42.5 centimeters wide, and 50 centimeters deep). The box would be made of a clear plastic material known as "lexan," and its back wall would be marked with black grid lines so that the position of the insects during flight could be accurately observed and recorded. A small digital timer would also be attached to the back wall to provide a means of timing the insects' flight behavior.

Todd's original design for the flight chamber had included canisters in which the insects would be stored until it was time for the experiment. In the new design, storage was handled in a different way. Jerry and Todd planned the box so that its volume could be reduced for storing the insects, then expanded for flight observation and filming. They did this by attaching plunger-like arms to an interior horizontal wall so that it could be moved up and down. As the wall moved, it increased the volume at one end of the chamber and decreased it at the other.

During the time when the experiment was stored in the shuttle locker, the insects would be confined in a small area at one end of the chamber. When the astronauts were ready to film the insects in flight, they would simply pull up on the plungers and expand the volume of the area so that the insects would have enough room to fly.

After completing the new design, Jerry and Todd began to build a prototype or mock-up of the flight chamber. Sometimes prototypes are scaled-down versions of the real thing, but Todd and

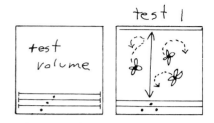

Above and opposite: Todd's sketches for a new flight chamber

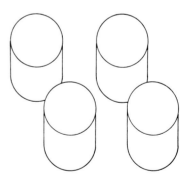

The storage cannisters in the original design were replaced by a new method of storage.

50

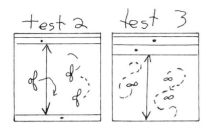

test 2   test 3

Jerry wanted to build this one to actual size so that they could put live insects in the chamber and see how (or if) they would fly. At the same time, Bob Peterson hoped to test the equipment that would be used to film the insects in the chamber.

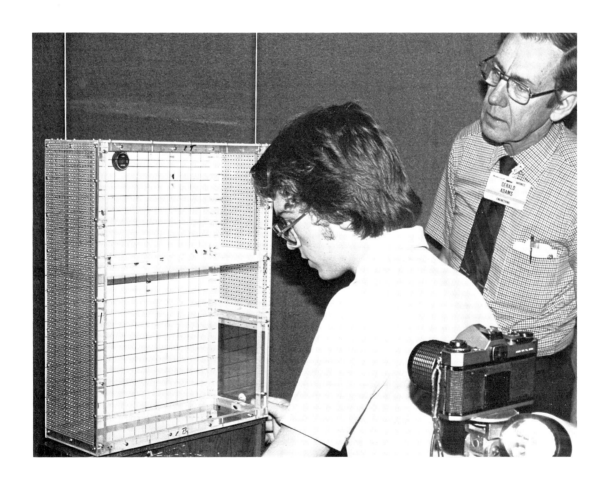

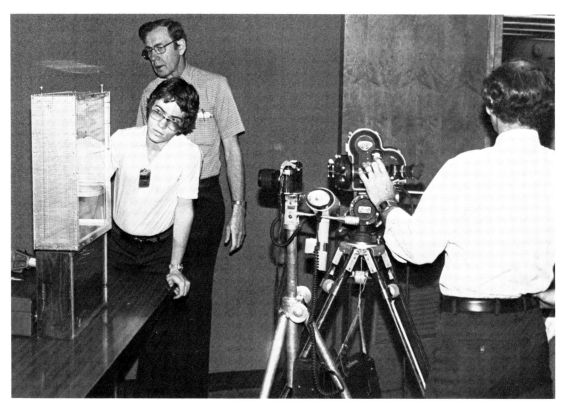

Todd and Jerry Adams (left) get ready to test the prototype.

The prototype was finished during the second week in November, right on schedule. Now it was ready for a test run, to be conducted at the Honeywell Avionics facility in Minneapolis. The "laboratory" was an ordinary conference room with overhead fluorescent light fixtures and a temperature of 70 degrees Fahrenheit (about 21 degrees Celsius).

Todd and Jerry put the prototype flight chamber on a table in the center of the room, while Honeywell photographer Ray Roberts set up 16mm motion picture cameras and 35mm still cameras on tripods in front of it. Also on the scene was Ken Bush of Honeywell's video services, who would record the whole test on video tape.

A video camera (right) is used to record the test.

Todd had brought some common houseflies to use as test subjects. When everything was ready, he released several flies into the small area in the box, using a door built into the side. The cameras began to roll as Todd pulled up on the plungers and the volume of space for flight grew larger. But the flies refused to cooperate. They hung on to the smooth plastic surface of the box, unwilling to fly. When Todd tapped the box with his finger, a single fly took off and flew only a short distance.

"Maybe it's too cool in the room," Todd said. He got out an everyday hair dryer, brought for just this purpose, and used it to warm the inside of the box. There was more flight activity, but it seemed to be caused only by the motion of the air. When the dryer stopped, flight stopped.

Todd was disappointed by the results of the test, but he had gained valuable information from it. He and Jerry Adams reported to Bob Peterson that this type of expandable box was just not practical as a flight chamber for the insects. The plunger arms were clumsy and hard to manage. The door in the side of the box was difficult to open and awkward to use when putting the insects into the chamber.

Todd had also learned some things about filming his experiment. The photographs taken in the test session were affected by light bouncing off the side of the box. These results demonstrated that the angle of the cameras in relation to the box was as important as the amount and source of the light.

Above: Todd pulls up on the plungers that enlarge the flight chamber. Below: He warms up the insects with a hair dryer.

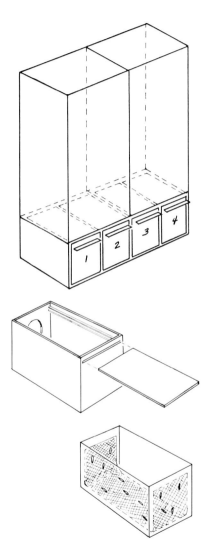

Drawings of Flight Chamber Number 2

The first trial was over and it had resulted in a good number of errors, but Todd and Jerry were eager to try again. After conferring with Bob Peterson, they began the design of Flight Chamber Number 2.

This second container was going to be given a real test aboard a mock-up of the space shuttle at Johnson Space Center in Houston, Texas. The test would have to yield better results than the first one if Todd was going to make STS-3. The tight schedule was getting tighter by the minute. Then, late in November, NASA announced that, because of technical problems, the third flight of the shuttle would be postponed until March 22, 1982. Todd could still make it!

By the first week in December, the second box was designed and one prototype built. This container was made of lexan, like the first one, but the plungers had been eliminated as well as the access door in the side. Instead of using an expandable chamber for storage, Todd had added four drawer compartments in one end of the container where the insects would be confined until released by the crew for observation and filming. A tool to pull open the small drawers was attached to the side of the box. Another change in this version of the flight container was its division into two equal vertical compartments, Chambers A and B, by a wall of clear lexan and screen. Each compartment had a digital timer attached to the back wall.

By December 8, the second box had been shipped to Johnson Space Center in Houston, and

Todd and Bob Peterson were on hand to conduct the test with the help of John Jackson and other NASA personnel. NASA photographer Donald Yeates would film the experiment using the same wall-mounted 16mm camera that would be used in space. The insect subjects for this second test were flies and moths supplied by Dr. Norm Leppla, an entomologist at the U.S. Department of Agriculture in Gainesville, Florida. Dr. Leppla had shipped the insects to Houston by plane to see if they could survive a journey on earth before sending them off into space.

Todd was excited about testing his experiment in a mock-up that was an exact replica of the space shuttle. This was a big change from the conference room that had been the setting of the first test. In the mock-up, he could go through the very same steps that the astronauts would go through when they conducted the experiment.

The first step was to put the flight chamber into the shuttle locker to make sure that it would fit. Then Todd removed the box from the locker just as the astronauts would and attached it to the wall of the orbiter middeck. He used the little tool on the side of the box to open one of the insect compartments in Chamber B. Nothing happened—no insects came out. When Todd tapped on the compartment, a couple of moths finally emerged. The cameras rolled, and Todd opened a drawer in Chamber A to let out some flies. As in the first test, there was very little flight activity. The insects clung to the screen and to the tops and sides of the metal compartments.

The second flight chamber included four drawers in which the insects would be stored.

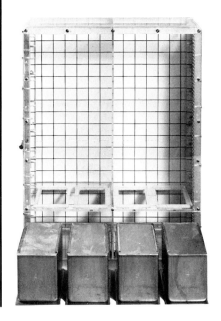

By tapping the side of the flight chamber, Todd could stimulate some flight, but it wasn't enough to get good pictures.

Again, the test was not what Todd called a success, but he had learned still more about how to turn his theory into reality. After studying the results of the test, Todd, Bob Peterson, and Jerry

Todd and Bob Peterson show the prototype of the second flight chamber to NASA education specialist Jim Poindexter inside the shuttle mock-up at Johnson Space Center.

Adams concluded that this version of the flight chamber had to be simplified still further. The division of the container into two separate chambers was a practical feature, but the storage drawers just didn't work. The drawers would have to be eliminated and the insects kept in the chamber

After attaching the flight chamber to the wall of the mock-up, Todd opens one of the insect compartments.

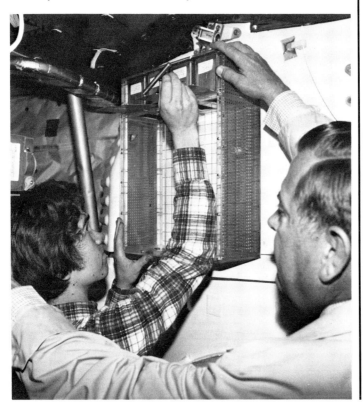

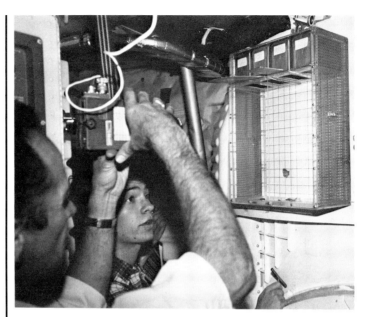

A few insects emerge to have their pictures taken.

itself instead of housing them in separate containers and releasing them in space. This would cut down on the amount of crew involvement; it would also increase the flying volume of the container and perhaps the flight activity. The insects' reluctance to fly was turning out to be a real problem, but Bob Peterson thought that there might be more flight activity in weightlessness than there had been so far in the earth-gravity tests.

The second test had also shown that the wall-mounted motion picture camera was going to be

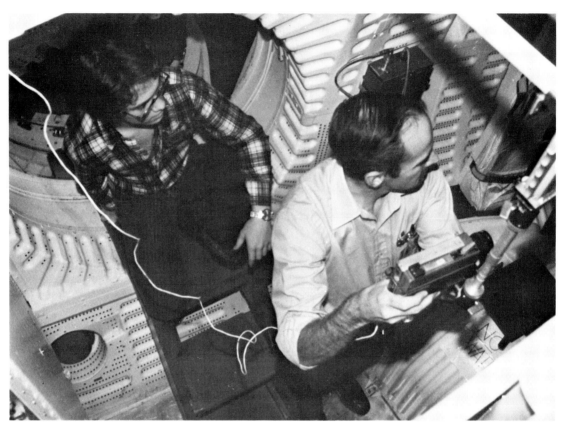

Donald Yeates, NASA photographer, experiments with the wall-mounted camera and lenses that will be used to film the insects.

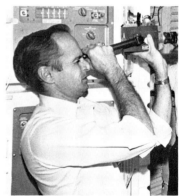

a problem. For one thing, it took too much crew time to fasten the camera to the wall of the shuttle. Also, because of the camera's fixed position, it was difficult to get close-ups of the insects with the lenses that would be on board the shuttle.

Todd and his advisors decided that they would have to ask the astronauts to hold the camera in their hands while filming. A few weeks later, the camera-mounting problem was solved when the STS-3 crew suggested using a video camera instead of the 16mm motion picture camera. It would be lighter and easier to handle. Even better, a video camera would make it possible for Todd and the rest of the world to watch as the crew conducted the experiment and beamed it down to earth via television satellite.

One final problem revealed by the test was that the box was difficult to remove from the drawer in the shuttle locker. The addition of handles on the side would make it easier for the astronauts to pull it up and out of the drawer.

When Todd went over the list of changes needed on the flight chamber, he became impatient. Setting up a scientific experiment was turning out to be a lot more complicated than he had ever imagined. Bob Roberts reminded him, "This is the way experiments are done, Todd. Trial and error. . . trial and error."

It was now the week before Christmas, and Todd was ready to design the third and, he hoped, final version of the flight chamber. John Jackson of NASA encouraged the Todd/Honeywell team to keep working fast in order to make the third flight of the space shuttle in March.

By mid-January 1982, Todd, Jerry, and Bob had the final design of the flight chamber completed. This was the simplest of all the plans. The small drawers in Version Number 2 had been eliminated,

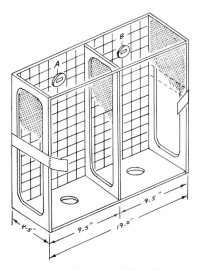

The design for the third and final flight chamber

allowing for storage of the insects in the container itself. The container was divided into two vertical chambers, as in the second version, and its back wall was equipped with grid lines and digital timers. Provisions were also made to fit the container with feeders holding food for the insects if this should prove necessary. (Feeders were eventually added.)

This version of the flight chamber included cylinders designed to hold food for the insects.

Design Number 3 was simple, practical, and flexible. A flight chamber constructed according to this plan should do the job. In fact, Todd and Jerry Adams were going to build not one flight chamber but four identical ones. One chamber would be used for the experiment in the shuttle, another for the control group of insects on earth. The other two chambers were spares that could be substituted in case something happened to the first two.

Jerry Adams with the four flight chambers built for the experiment

Todd, Bob Peterson, and Bob Moulton display the insect flight chamber at a press conference.

Early in February, Todd and Bob Peterson announced to NASA that the flight chamber was ready to fly. After weeks of hard work, half of the experiment was completed. Now, with the right crew of "insectronauts," Todd's "Insect in Flight Motion Study" could be ready for the next space shuttle mission.

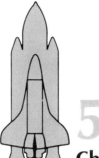

5

Choosing the "Insectronauts"

Selecting the right crew of insectronauts for the experiment was as big a job as designing the flight chamber, and it had to be done at the same time. During the weeks and months that Todd worked with Jerry Adams on the box design, he was also conferring with Bob Peterson and other advisors about the choice of insects. Both parts of the experiment were equally important, and both had to be planned with the same kind of care and attention to detail.

Like the design of the flight chamber, the work of choosing the insects got underway right after the design review meeting in September. As a result of the discussion among the team members at the meeting, Todd had a better idea of the requirements that would have to be filled in selecting the right subjects for his experiment. He described some of these requirements in his final report: "The criteria for selection of the insect species to be studied included such things as physical size, lifespan, food requirements and the ability to fly well in the volume provided within the insect flight box used in the experiment."

As Bob Buda had pointed out at the design review meeting, lifespan was one of the most important things to be considered in choosing insects. If Todd's subjects died in space before the experiment could be conducted, then all his work would have been for nothing. Todd and his advisors decided that they could use only those insect species that lived for at least nine days in their adult stage.

Todd picked a nine-day lifespan because it would allow the experiment to be conducted on any day of the seven-day shuttle mission. If the scheduled day of the test was changed, there would still be living subjects. A nine-day lifespan also provided a cushion in case the shuttle launch was postponed for several days.

Dr. Norm Leppla, the entomologist with the U.S. Department of Agriculture, gave Todd an idea for an unusual insurance policy that would guarantee living subjects for his experiment. Dr. Leppla suggested that Todd consider using insects in the pupal stage as well as adults. The insect pupae would complete their development and emerge as adults in space, ready to try their brand-new wings. This would provide a young group of flying insects whose behavior could be compared with that of the older adults in the experiment.

In addition to lifespan, the physical size of the

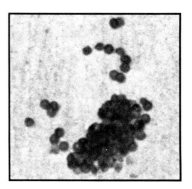

Eggs

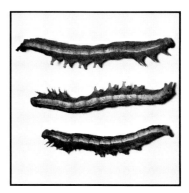

Larvae

Pupae

Moths, flies, bees, and many other kinds of insects develop through a complicated process known as metamorphosis. During the pupal stage of metamorphosis, the insect larva, enclosed in a cocoon or pupal shell, changes into an adult insect.

Adults

insects was an important consideration. Since Todd was going to use photography and video tape to collect data for his experiment, the insects had to be large enough to show up clearly in the filmed record. On the other hand, it was necessary to choose insects that would be able to fly normally even in the small volume of the flight chamber.

Another key requirement was the kind of food that the insects would eat. Insects with short life-spans often consume nothing in their adult forms, but insects that live for nine days as adults would need food during that time. Since there was going to be more than one species of insect used in the experiment, it would simplify things if all

67

could have the same food. It wouldn't be a good idea to send a plant eater into space along with a meat eater. Similar eating habits would simplify food requirements and also the equipment needed to supply food and water on board the shuttle.

One special consideration that Todd had to keep in mind while choosing insects for his experiment was the extreme changes in gravity that his insectronauts would be subjected to. While in space, the insects would be in zero gravity, but during the shuttle launch and landing, they would experience as much as seven times the normal force of gravity on earth. Todd did not know— nor did anyone else—what kinds of insects might be able to survive these terrible "G" forces, but he could try to increase the chance that at least some of his subjects would survive. As he wrote in his report, "Since any single species of insect could have died prior to data collection (e.g., may not have survived launch accelerations), the success of the experiment was better ensured by using more than one species."

In addition to the special requirements of an insect experiment conducted in space, Todd had to meet the same careful standards used in any scientific experiment involving animals. He had to be sure that he could get healthy insects raised under laboratory conditions so that they were as much alike as possible. The more similar the insects within each species were to each other, the more consistent the results of the experiment would be. If the behavior of the insects in space and those on earth was different, then the differ-

The insects in Todd's experiment would experience as much as seven times the normal force of gravity during the shuttle launch.

Like all scientists, Todd wanted to use insects bred in a laboratory so that they were as much alike as possible.

ence could be traced to the one major variable, weightlessness, and not to differences in the insects' individual characteristics.

Armed with their long list of requirements, Todd and Bob Peterson began their search for the best possible crew of insectronauts. Their first contact was Dr. Bill Williams of NASA's Ames Research Center in California, who was assigned as Todd's advisor. Dr. Williams not only knew a great deal about insects but had also co-authored a paper just two years earlier about the effects of weightlessness on the flight of moths.

Dr. Williams' paper was based on an experiment conducted aboard a NASA airplane that simulated zero gravity in the only way possible on earth.

The plane flew in a pattern of sharp ascents and descents, and as it reached the top of one of its steep climbs, there was a brief moment of weightlessness before the descent began. Dr. Williams' moths were in zero gravity for only these short periods of time, but the scientist was able to make some observations that Todd found helpful in planning his own much longer experiment.

With help and advice from Dr. Williams, Dr. Dale Habeck of the Department of Entomology and Nematology of the University of Florida, Gainesville, and Dr. Norm Leppla, Todd selected the velvetbean caterpillar moth as the first member of his insectronaut crew. Dr. Leppla, who would supply the moths for Todd's experiment, suggested this species because it lived at least nine days as an adult. Velvetbean caterpillar moths also met the other requirements that Todd had established. They could fly in the space provided, they were not fussy eaters, and they didn't need a great deal of food for a seven-day mission. The moths were not predators so they wouldn't cause problems with the other insects, and they were large enough to provide good pictures.

Todd's velvetbean caterpillar moths would be the first adult moths and moth pupae ever launched into space. Some moth eggs had already made the trip. In 1973, NASA had sent a container of gypsy moth eggs into space on *Skylab.* When they were returned to earth, some of the eggs hatched and continued their development, but Todd's moths would be the first ones to emerge as adults in a weightless environment.

The velvetbean caterpillar moth

One of the unknowns of the experiment was whether or not the moths would be able to "inflate" their wings after emergence as they do on earth. When an adult moth or butterfly comes out of its cocoon, its wings are small and crumpled. The insects must force body fluids through the vein networks in its wings in order to expand them to their full size. Todd's experiment would show whether moths could go through this important step of their development in zero gravity.

After choosing the velvetbean caterpillar moth, Todd and Bob Peterson went on to select its companions for the space journey. Most of the insects on Todd's original list of choices had already been rejected as unsuitable, but one still remained in the running—the common housefly. Todd and his advisors took another look at the housefly and decided that it met all the requirements of size, lifespan, and food needs. The housefly became the second member of the insectronaut crew.

Todd's original plans for using houseflies included the possibility of removing the halteres on some of the insects to compare their flight behavior to other flies with the little gyroscopes intact. Now Todd and Bob Peterson agreed that they would not remove any of the flies' halteres because that would introduce another variable, making the experiment more difficult to record and analyze.

Todd planned to get his houseflies from Dr. Phil Morgan at the Insects Affecting Man and Animals Research Laboratory in Gainesville, but as the date of the launch approached, Dr. Morgan's fly

The housefly with its unique halteres (indicated by arrow) was the second kind of insect chosen for the experiment.

Dr. David Pimentel and his fly colony

colony began to develop some problems. The flies weren't as healthy as they should have been, and it was decided that another fly colony would have to be found.

After some frantic searching, Todd got the name of Dr. David Pimentel, an entomologist at Cornell University in New York. He called Dr. Pimentel and explained his experiment and his predicament. The entomologist agreed to supply fly puparia from his colony, which he described as "robust."

Now the second insect species for the experiment was selected and ready to go.

The decision had been made to include only one other kind of insect, and Todd wanted to consider the kind he knew best, the honeybee. Dr. Harry Laidlaw, an entomologist retired from the University of California, helped Todd and Bob Peterson in this final selection. Dr. Laidlaw suggested that the worker honeybee would have a better chance of survival outside the hive than the drones and the queen, the other members of the honeybee community. The lifespan of the worker was adequate, its size was right, and its food requirement no different from the moths and houseflies. But there was one drawback. Worker honeybees had stingers and knew how to use them. Stinging bees on the shuttle could endanger the astronauts and their mission.

The solution to this problem came from Mel Coplin, NASA employee and beekeeper. He suggested that the bees' stingers be clipped. Mel experimented and found that he could clip one-thousandth of an inch off the stingers without damaging the bees or causing illness. His colony of bees was healthy, and he would be happy to provide subjects for the experiment, minus the working parts of their stingers.

Todd's insect selection was complete, and he had a reliable source for each of the three groups: velvetbean caterpillar moths, common houseflies, and worker honeybees. A delivery schedule for the insectronauts was set up for the week of the launch. Everything was ready to go.

STS-3 astronauts Jack Lousma (left) and Gordon Fullerton (right) get their first look at Todd's experiment.

On February 22, 1982, Todd carried a flight-worthy insect flight chamber to Johnson Space Center, where he met astronauts Gordon Fullerton and Jack Lousma and discussed his experiment in a briefing for the press. At that briefing, NASA announced that Todd Nelson's "Insect in Flight Motion Study" would be on board the third mission of the space shuttle *Columbia* in March. His was the first student experiment ready, and it would be the "first to fly."

During a briefing at Kennedy Space Center, Bob Peterson (center) told members of the press that Todd Nelson's "Insect in Flight Motion Study" would be the first to fly.

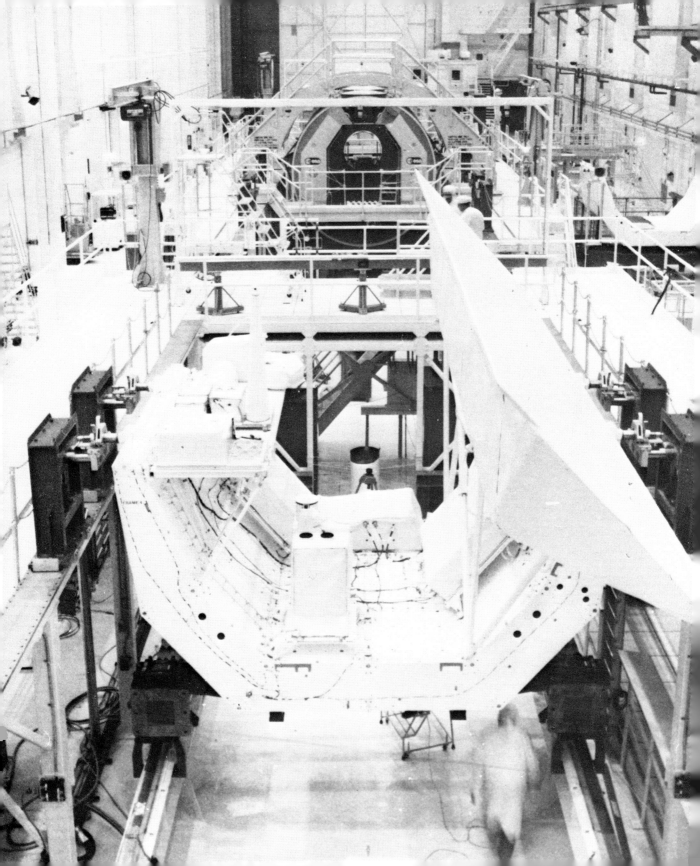

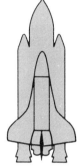

6 Insects in Space

The flight chambers were designed and built, the insect subjects chosen and ready for delivery. The launch date of STS-3 was exactly one month away. Now Todd, Bob Peterson, and Jerry Adams had to plan the final stage of the "Insect in Flight Motion Study" experiment.

These final plans were complicated because Todd's experiment would include two sets of observations—one conducted in space by the astronauts, the other, a control test that Todd would run at the Johnson Space Center in Texas. Careful schedules had to be set up to make sure that the flight chambers and the insectronauts would be at the right places at the right times.

A week before the launch, all the plans were set in motion. Two of the four complete flight chambers were shipped to John Jackson at Johnson

A "clean room" at Kennedy Space Center in Cape Canaveral, Florida

The mission operations control room at Johnson Space Center, Houston, Texas

Space Center (JSC) for final NASA inspection, approval, and packaging. One box was then sent by NASA to Kennedy Space Center (KSC) for the space flight, while the other was held at JSC for the control group of insects. Todd and Bob Peterson would take the two extra boxes with them to Cape Canaveral and then on to Johnson Space Center. Because those boxes would not be going on a manned space flight, they did not need to pass a strict inspection.

The insect passengers had their own schedules. Two sets of each species of insect were to be sent to both Kennedy and Johnson space centers.

Todd would load the insects into the space flight chamber at KSC before he went to JSC to conduct the control observations. The control flight chamber would be loaded by NASA personnel at JSC.

Several days before the launch, the human participants in the experiment began to appear on the scene. Todd, his parents, his science teacher, Bob Roberts, and various Honeywell advisors arrived at Cape Canaveral on March 19 after receiving a rousing send-off from Todd's high school band. They were met at Kennedy Space Center

Reporters snapped pictures and the high school band played when Todd and his family left Minnesota for Kennedy Space Center.

by Alan Ladwig, NASA manager of the Shuttle Student Involvement Project, who was working with other NASA officials to iron out final details for the experiment.

John Jackson arrived the next morning from Johnson Space Center, bringing the flight chamber that would go aboard the shuttle. The box had been thoroughly inspected and cleaned by NASA at JSC. Each screw, bit of glue, even the batteries in the little timers attached to the back wall of the box had been checked to be sure that they met NASA specifications for a manned space flight. At KSC, John Jackson turned the flight chamber over to a NASA payload integration team. It would be stored in a sterile room along with the astronauts' space suits until the insects arrived and it was time to load the experiment.

The first of the insectronauts to arrive were the houseflies, sent by Dr. Pimentel from Cornell. They came in a small shipping tube addressed to Todd Nelson at Day's Inn, Titusville, Florida. Todd picked up the package at the motel desk on the morning of March 21 and took it to his room without trying to explain to the receptionist what the tube contained.

Mel Coplin sent his honeybees (minus stingers) from the Coplin Bee Farm, Arcadia, Texas, to Cape Canaveral by way of Johnson Space Center. The bees were loaded on a NASA jet that landed at Patrick Air Force Base near Canaveral on the afternoon of March 21. John Jackson and Bob Peterson picked up the tiny wooden boxes and took them to Kennedy Space Center.

Alan Ladwig

Dr. Norm Leppla's van, nicknamed the Space Moth Delivery Vehicle, pulled up at the KSC guard gate about 8 P.M. that night. Dr. Leppla explained to the armed security guard that he had brought some "bugs for the shuttle." The guard told him politely to "turn around and get away from Kennedy Space Center." Contacted by phone, John

Dr. Norm Leppla (left) and the Space Moth Delivery Vehicle

Jackson and Bob Peterson came to the rescue, explaining to the guard that Dr. Leppla was, in fact, delivering insects that were going up in the shuttle the next morning. Everyone had a good laugh about the incident, but nerves were becoming tense as launch time approached.

NASA's schedule called for the flight chamber, with its insect cargo, to be taken aboard the shuttle at 11 P.M., March 21. At 9 P.M., Todd began preparations for loading his insects into the chamber, aided by Dr. Leppla and Jerry Adams. First, the two feeding containers were each filled with one fluid ounce of sugar solution and placed in the box, one in Chamber A and the other in Chamber B. The digital timers on the back wall were checked for proper time and date display. Now Todd was ready for the insectronauts.

In Chamber A, he loaded 12 common housefly puparia, 12 male velvetbean caterpillar moths, and 12 female velvetbean caterpillar moths. In Chamber B, he put 14 worker honeybees, 12 male velvetbean caterpillar moth pupae, and 12 female velvetbean caterpillar moth pupae. Six each of the male and female moth pupae were attached to small pieces of screen that were in turn fastened to the screens inside the box. The other 12 moth pupae and all the fly puparia were not fastened down; they would float freely once the box was in space.

The placement of insects in the chamber had been planned carefully to provide the most information possible from the experiment. Adult moths were separated from pupae so Todd could observe

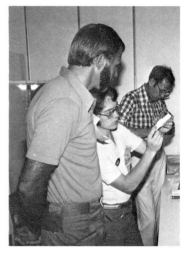

Todd, Jerry Adams, and Norm Leppla prepare the insects for loading in the flight chamber.

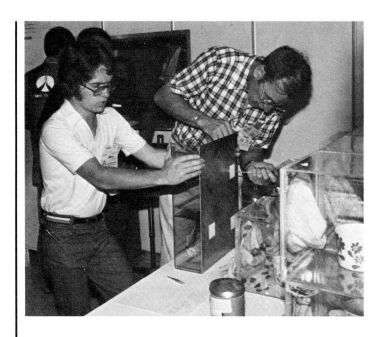

Jerry Adams removes the back of the chamber so that the insects can be inserted.

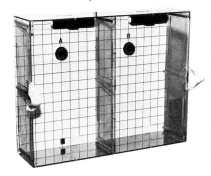

The insects were carefully divided between chambers A and B so that there would be flight activity in both parts of the container.

any differences in flight behavior between the adults and the young moths that emerged in space. The fly puparia and the moth pupae had been put in separate chambers along with the adult insects so that there would be flight activity in both chambers in case the immature insects were unable to complete their development. Both the fly puparia and the moth pupae were scheduled to produce adults one or two days after the shuttle launch.

The loading process took nearly two hours. It was close to 11 P.M. when a NASA team put the flight chamber in a stowage locker tray, wrapped

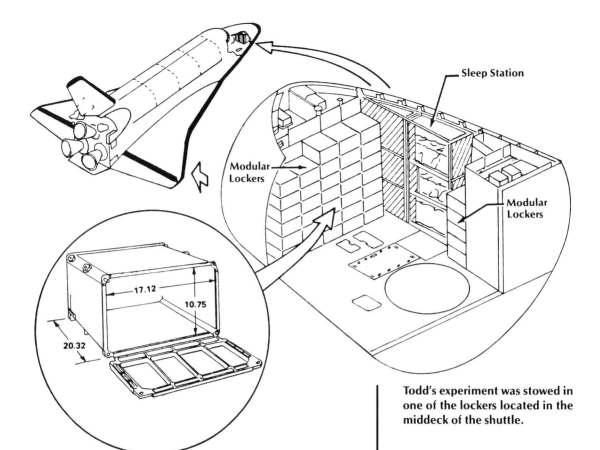

Sleep Station

Modular
Lockers

17.12

10.75

20.32

Modular
Lockers

Todd's experiment was stowed in one of the lockers located in the middeck of the shuttle.

the whole package in a clear, sterile plastic film, and put it on a scale. The combined weight of box and tray was 6 pounds, 14 ounces (about 3 kilograms), well under the maximum weight limit. After NASA officials signed the final approval forms in the shuttle logbook, the flight chamber package was taken to a waiting vehicle that would deliver it to the *Columbia* launch pad. There it would be stowed in shuttle locker MA9L to await tomorrow's launch.

Many of the scientific experiments carried on *Columbia* were packaged in the Space Sciences pallet, shown here being lowered into the shuttle's payload bay during pre-mission processing.

More than a month before the launch date, the STS-3 shuttle was moved from the Vehicle Assembly Building to Launch Pad 39A by a slow-moving crawler-transporter.

Left: The STS-3 crew—Commander Jack Lousma (left) and Pilot Gordon Fullerton (right). Above: The *Columbia* **is on its way.**

At 11 A.M. the next morning, the space shuttle *Columbia* roared into space and, with it, Todd's "Insect in Flight Motion Study." Watching the launch with his parents and friends, Todd wondered how the insectronauts were surviving the tremendous gravitational forces created by the shuttle's lift-off. At the Johnson Space Center in Houston, NASA workers responsible for setting up the control part of the experiment were making sure that the control insects were experiencing the same crushing forces as their high-flying relatives.

Ruben Zavala and Ralph Drexel were the NASA employees who had come up with a device that would subject the control insects to the same G forces experienced by the insects in the shuttle. Working evenings and weekends, the two men had built a turntable powered by a used washing machine motor. Attached to the turntable was a long arm designed to hold the control flight chamber. When the motor was turned on, the turntable spun the chamber around and around. The faster the box was spun, the greater the G forces exerted on it.

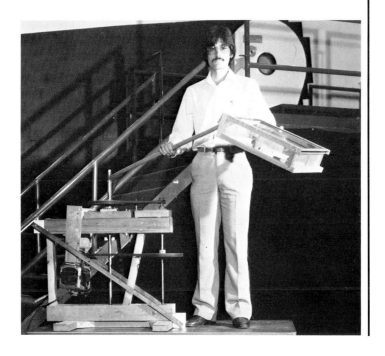

Ruben Zavala with the machine he created to duplicate the G forces of launch and landing.

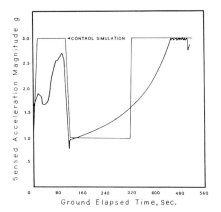

This chart compares the G forces experienced by the two sets of insects in the experiment.

With the help of this unique machine, NASA employees at JSC would be able to make the control test as much like the space experiment as possible. At the time of the launch, Ruben Zavala took the control flight chamber out of the locker of the shuttle mock-up where it had been stored after loading. Ruben mounted the chamber on the arm of the turntable and turned on the motor. Using a NASA graph that showed how G forces increase and decrease during the launch, he varied the speed of his machine to duplicate the pattern of those changing forces. Inside the chamber, the control insects experienced the same powerful gravitational pull as the insects blasting into space on the shuttle.

On March 24, 55 hours after the shuttle launch, astronauts Gordon Fullerton and Jack Lousma took the flight chamber out of locker MA9L, removed it from the tray, and attached it to a wall of the middeck with velcro fasteners. Back on earth, Todd went through exactly the same motions in the shuttle mock-up at Johnson Space Center. Both the space insects and the earth insects seemed to have survived the extreme G forces without any noticeable damage. When the astronauts attached the flight chamber to the wall, they could see the insectronauts moving around inside. The control insects were clinging to the bottom surfaces of their chamber, held down securely by the force of gravity.

There was not much flight activity in either chamber, and both Todd and the astronauts had to tap the boxes to get the insects moving. The

Jack Lousma observes the flight activity of the space insects.

flight behavior in both experiments was carefully recorded on film and video tape, and detailed notes were taken. As Todd conducted the control observations in the shuttle mock-up at JSC, he was able to watch the space experiment on television. It was a great moment for the young scientist.

90

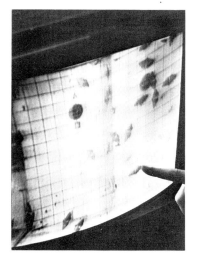

On March 27, during Day Six of the flight, Commander Lousma and Pilot Fullerton gave Todd an unexpected bonus when they performed his experiment a second time. Todd got a personal message from Commander Lousma, who signed off by saying, "Hope you learned a lot from this, Todd."

Back on earth, Todd, Bob Peterson, Alan Ladwig, and a NASA employee watch on television as the astronauts conduct the experiment in space.

Todd Nelson's experiment was in good scientific company on STS-3, called by NASA the Pathfinder mission because it prepared the way for future flights and experiments. One of the experiments carried on the flight was the plasma diagnostics package, shown here held by a remote manipulator arm (left) on the outside of the space ship. The package was designed to test the effects of *Columbia's* electrical fields on plasma (ionized gas).

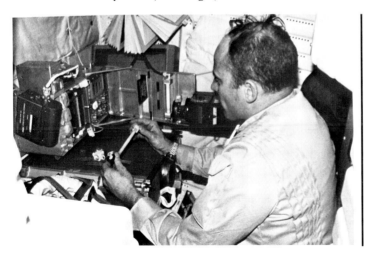

Jack Lousma prepares an experiment that will use an electrical field to separate human cells.

The *Columbia* makes a perfect landing at White Sands Test Facility in New Mexico.

Astronauts Fullerton and Lousma leave the shuttle at the end of their eight-day mission.

The astronauts went on to other experiments for the rest of their mission, called by NASA "the busiest and most successful" of the experimental shuttle flights. At 11:05 A.M. Eastern Standard Time, March 30, 1982, Commander Lousma and Pilot Fullerton landed *Columbia* on Northrup Air Strip at White Sands Test Facility in New Mexico. Within an hour of the landing, Todd's experiment was removed from the orbiter, enclosed in an airtight container, and placed aboard a T-38 jet for delivery to Johnson Space Center. Like the astronauts, the insectronauts had to be tested and examined thoroughly after their long journey in space.

From the first press conference in August 1981 (above) up to the day of the launch (below), Todd and his experiment received a great deal of attention from the media. Newspapers, magazines, television stations, radio stations, and news services from all over the world wrote about, talked about, interviewed, and took pictures of the 18-year-old scientist from Rose Creek, Minnesota, who was going to put "bugs on the shuttle."

On the day of the launch, Todd was interviewed on national television by Tom Brokaw (top left) and Diane Sawyer (center left). He also appeared on the "Good Morning, America" show, where he talked with David Hartman (right) and former astronaut James McDivitt (center). At the launch site, Todd was interviewed by a reporter from *Odyssey*, a science magazine for young people (top right).

Above and below: Cartoons about Todd's experiment were featured in newspapers all over the world.

March 5, 1982

Dear Cols. Lousma and Fullerton,

Please don't swat Todd's bugs! It would hurt Todd's feelings. They are part of his experiment. We are curious to know how the bugs fly with no gravity. If they get out of the boxes, you could use a net to catch them.

We can hardly wait for the blast off! We hope you have a good ride in the space shuttle. We'll be watching you on TV and we'll wave at you. We are proud of you and Todd.

Love,
The Southland
Kindergarten
Rose Creek, Mn.

Stephanie
Scott
Janet
Amy
Jara
Christen
Adam
Andy B.
Mike
Randy
Crystal
Robin
Joshua
Melissa
Diane
Greg
Andy
Mark
Jamie
Matthew
Linsey
Mrs. Lynda Gillis

Lisa S.
Beth
Clinton
Andy R.
Matt
Tommy
Brandon
Lisa
Gary
Mike
Michelle
Heath
Jason
Jill
Darin
Andrea
Greg U
Eddy
Jed
Jason R
Stacy
Mrs. Sharon Loeschen

Jill
Angie
Kathy o.
Denise
Mike V.
Joshua
Stefani
Justin
Jorine
Ercle
Mandy
Kerie
Kristle
Sara
Tyja
Tony
Heather

A kindergarten class in Todd's hometown of Rose Creek, Minnesota, sent this letter to the astronauts, asking them to take good care of Todd's "bugs."

97

This picture of the wing of a honeybee used in Todd's experiment was taken with a scanning electron microscope at NASA's Ames Research Center.

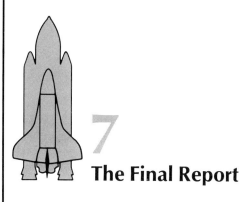

7

The Final Report

Todd's lesson in the scientific method didn't end with the completion of the experiment and the landing of the space shuttle. According to the rules of the Shuttle Student Involvement Project, he had to conduct an analysis of the data he had collected and then write a final report. The report was to be finished within 90 days of the experiment and submitted to NASA and NSTA for review and publication.

Bob Roberts and Bob Peterson helped Todd to sift through all the notes, observations, and comments made by people who had seen the experiment. He also reviewed NASA video tapes and photos, reread papers written by entomologists and other experimenters, and listened to what the astronauts themselves had to say. Then he drafted his final report.

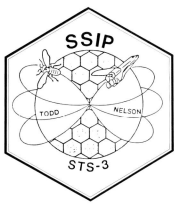

The symbol that Todd designed for his SSIP experiment appeared on the first page of his final report.

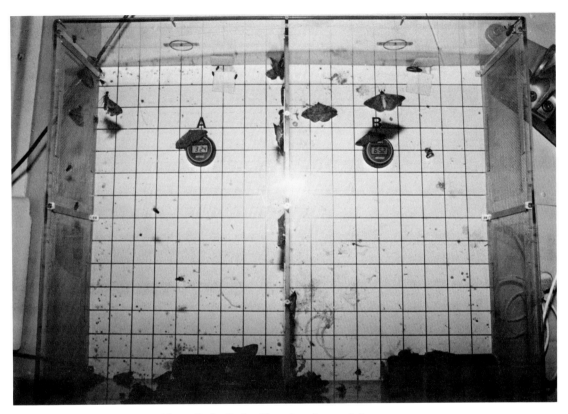

In preparing his report, Todd studied all the filmed and taped records of the experiment.

Todd's report documented the entire experiment. It described the planning and preparations, the choice of insects, the equipment used, the procedures followed, and, of course, the results. The results made up the major part of the report, the part on which Todd worked the hardest. He had collected a great deal of information, and interpreting it was a big job. In the report's conclusion, Todd made a general comment on what he had learned: "The results from this insect flight motion study may have raised more questions than they have answered." It was the same comment that many professional scientists have made about the results of their experiments.

Although Todd's results were not conclusive, they did seem to support his final hypothesis: "Flying insects should encounter problems in pitching orientation in zero gravity depending on the type of flight control mechanism of the insects observed." The space insects did have problems in pitching orientation—the horizontal position of their bodies in flight—and the problems did seem to be related to the differences among the three kinds of insects. Todd summarized the results in these words:

> Comparisons of the zero-g flight responses of the three species of insects suggest that the flies were most able to control their flight and body orientations. The moths appeared to be somewhat poorer at controlling their flight and body orientations than the flies. The bees appeared to be unable to control their flight in zero-g conditions and they were observed to mostly float about randomly in the flight box.

As Todd had anticipated, the houseflies turned out to be the best navigators in zero gravity— that is, when they chose to fly at all.

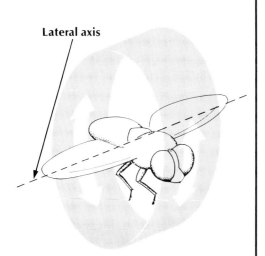

Lateral axis

Pitch is the movement of an object in flight around its lateral axis. Todd's final hypothesis was designed to test the effects of zero gravity on the pitching orientation of flying insects.

Ten of 12 flies aboard STS-3 were observed to have emerged from puparia by the third day of the flight (at about 55 hours after launch). Their activity in zero-g consisted primarily of walking on the interior surfaces of the flight box. When they flew, they tended to fly only briefly (with a maximum observed flight duration of four seconds). During the flight observations, the flies appeared able to control their motion in all three of their body axes (pitch, yaw, and roll) and appeared to have no difficulty flying from point to point in the box. . . .

The flight activity of the moths in space was also brief, lasting less than ten seconds during each attempt by a moth. During flight, the body axis might be oriented in any direction. The moths' flight patterns were very

NUMBERS OF MOTHS AT VARIOUS BODY ORIENTATIONS ON THE FRONT PLANE OF THE INSECT FLIGHT BOX				
GRAVITY LEVEL (2)	BODY ORIENTATION (1)			
	HEAD UP	HEAD DOWN	HEAD RIGHT	HEAD LEFT
ZERO-G	17	20	18	3
ONE-G	8	0	0	0

The final report included this chart comparing the body positions of moths in the two flight containers during part of the experiment.

After the experiment, the velvet-bean caterpillar moths were sent to Dr. Norm Leppla for examination and furthur study. The picture below shows the containers holding the moths in Dr. Leppla's laboratory.

uncontrolled and would often "level off" to just maintaining position against the surface of the flight chamber.

The young moths that emerged during the shuttle mission flew as well as the old ones, although they tended to spend more time floating than their elders. All the moths, "like the flies, appeared to have no difficulty clinging to any of the interior surfaces of the flight box."

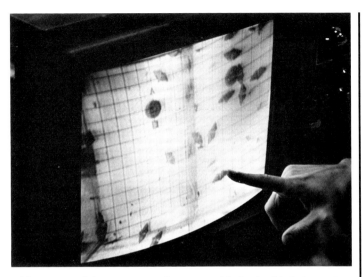

Video tapes of the space experiment provided valuable information about the flight behavior of the insects.

The worker honeybees experienced the most problems in the zero-gravity environment.

> The 14 bees aboard STS-3 were observed to walk only on the screen surface inside the flight box. They appeared to be unable to cling to the smooth plastic surfaces. Brief attempts at flight resulted in unstable paths, tumbling about their body axes. . . . In one case, two bees were observed on the screen together. Both bees left the screen, "hooked" together and spinning rapidly, which lasted for about 25 seconds. After separating, both bees went off spinning in

CONDITIONS OF INSECTS AS OBSERVED AT THE DEPARTMENT OF BIOLOGY, UNIVERSITY OF HOUSTON ON MARCH 31, 1982		CHAMBER A	CHAMBER B
ZERO-G BOX	NO. OF FLY PUPARIA EMERGED	10 OF 12	--
	NO. OF LIVE FLIES (ADULTS)	10 OF 10	--
	NO. OF MOTH PUPAE EMERGED	--	22 OF 24
	NO. OF LIVE MOTHS (ADULTS)	20 OF 24	15 OF 22
	NO. OF LIVE BEES (ADULTS)	--	0 OF 14
ONE-G BOX	NO. OF FLY PUPARIA EMERGED	12 OF 12	--
	NO. OF LIVE FLIES (ADULTS)	12 OF 12	--
	NO. OF MOTH PUPAE EMERGED	--	11 OF 22
	NO. OF LIVE MOTHS (ADULTS)	16 OF 24	6 OF 11
	NO. OF LIVE BEES (ADULTS)	--	5 OF 12

This chart from Todd's report shows the condition of the insects at the end of the experiment. Examination revealed that Chamber B of the control (one-G) box contained only 22 moth pupae instead of 24. The other two "pupae" turned out to be empty pupal cases that had been put into the chamber by mistake.

different directions. . . . Floating was observed for long durations and appeared to be a result of inability to cling to a smooth surface when [the bees] came into contact with it (with wingbeat ceasing at contact).

It seemed clear that the bees were the losers and the flies the winners in the competition for the best insectronauts. Todd did not find enough evidence to show that the flies' superior performance was due to their unique balancing organs, the halteres, but his experiment did seem to suggest this possibility. It was a possibility that could be explored in future experiments.

Todd's experiment had resulted in information that supported his hypothesis, but it had also produced results in other important areas. For instance, the experiment showed that both adult insects and pupae could withstand the G forces of launch and landing. The new adults were able to emerge successfully in a weightless environment whether they were free-floating or fastened down. After emergence, they proved able to expand their wings and fly, just like insects on earth.

One interesting observation on insect flight behavior in zero gravity came from the second, bonus experiment that the astronauts had conducted on Day Six of the mission. In looking at the video tape of this experiment and comparing it to the first one, Todd noticed something unusual:

> On the first test day in space (flight day 3), the lighting conditions were uniform throughout the box. The flight activity of all the insects was also observed throughout the flight box, with no apparent preference for any area.... The lighting conditions were different during the second test day in space (on flight day 6). The intensity was greatest

Above: A picture taken through a scanning electron microscope of the head of one of the shuttle bees. Below: This picture of a shuttle bee's wings shows some worn areas at the tips, which might have developed during the space flight.

in the upper third of the flight chamber. All moths exhibiting flight activity did so in the region of the brightest illumination.

The apparent attraction of the moths for the area of brightest light was interesting, but there was not enough data to interpret or analyze. This was another subject that would have to be studied in further experiments.

To aid scientists conducting such experiments, Todd included in his report some observations about designs of future "insect habitats for use

Feeding the insects and disposing of their waste material turned out to be problems in Todd's experiment.

in the zero-g environment of space" based on the problems that had developed in his experiment. Two of the major problems had to do with feeding and waste disposal.

All of the space bees and more than half of the earth bees were dead at the end of the experiment, and laboratory analysis showed that they probably died from lack of food. Dr. Shim Shimanuki of the U.S. Department of Agriculture Bioenvironmental Bee Laboratory in Beltsville, Maryland, examined four bees, two from the space flight and two from the control test. His finding showed that the bees were free of disease, that clipping the stingers didn't reduce their life span, and that the glue used to fasten the pupae to the screens hadn't harmed the bees. Dr. Shimanuki concluded that the sugar solution in the food supply was probably too weak to sustain the insects over the nine-day experiment.

The bees' feeding problem was made more complicated by the fact that they were unable to hold onto the smooth plastic surface of the box with their feet. This meant that they could not stay in one place long enough to get nourishment from the feeder. Based on these difficulties, Todd recommended that any future insect habitat in space should provide "a food/water source that be easily accessed by, and that will provide for the nutritional needs of, each of the insect species to be carried" and "textures of materials inside the habitat that will allow all species . . . to easily maintain resting positions on (or move about on) the surfaces in zero-g. The nature of the insects'

A fly's foot (above) is equipped with sticky tube-shaped structures, while a bee's foot (below) has only claws. The differences in the insects' feet help to explain why the bees were less successful than the flies in clinging to the smooth walls of the flight chamber.

feet must be considered in the selection of these materials."

Waste disposal in zero gravity turned out to be another unexpected problem. During the experiment in space, waste material produced by the insects floated around the flight chamber and collected on the walls instead of settling to the bottom as it would in normal gravity. The clutter caused by this debris made observation and filming of the insects less than ideal. Todd recommended that future space experiments include "some waste collection system to prevent floating debris and deposits on surfaces (especially if clear viewing and/or recording of insect activity is required.)"

Scientists in the future would learn as much from the problems that developed in Todd's experiment as they would from its successes. They would be able to build on his work and use it as a base in designing similar studies. As Todd wrote in his final report, his experiment had "opened up new and exciting areas for future research, which can add to what is already known about insect motion in zero-gravity." Todd Nelson's "Insect in Flight Motion Study" had become a part of the ongoing process of learning in which all scientists share.

Michelle Issel's experiment on the formation of crystals in zero gravity flew on STS-5 in November 1982.

8 Other SSIP Experiments

Todd Nelson's experiment was the first to fly, but it was soon followed by other student experiments in space. By the time that STS-6 was launched in February 1983, more than half of the first 10 SSIP winners had already had their experiments conducted aboard the space shuttle.

On June 27, 1982, STS-4 blasted off with astronauts Thomas Mattingly and Henry Hartsfield on board. In addition to their other duties, the two men were serving as subjects for experiments studying the effects of weightlessness on protein and mineral levels in the human body. The experiments were developed by two high school students, Amy Kusske of Long Beach, California, and Karla Hauersperger of Charlotte, North Carolina. Amy's work was sponsored by the McDonnell Douglas Corporation and Karla's by the Explorers Club.

Amy Kusske's STS-4 experiment tested the effects of diet and exercise on protein levels in the bodies of the astronauts on the shuttle mission. In this photograph, Amy is shown seated at the control panel of the shuttle flight trainer at Johnson Space Center.

During the week before the launch, the two young scientists spent hours with the astronauts, helping to plan their diets and to monitor their vital signs. In making their final reports, Karla and Amy compared the results of the pre-flight studies with the data on the astronauts' condition collected during and after the flight. Their experiments produced valuable new information about the effects of zero gravity on the human body.

STS-5, launched on November 11, 1982, set a NASA record for having the largest crew of any shuttle flight up to that time. Four astronauts flew on the mission, and they carried with them the experiments of three students—Michelle Issel of Wallingford, Connecticut; Aaron Gillette of Winter Haven, Florida; and Scott Thomas of Johnston, Pennsylvania.

Michelle Issel's experiment, which was sponsored by Hamilton Standard Corporation, was designed to study the formation of crystals in zero gravity. Michelle's triglycine sulfate crystal did grow during the shuttle flight but not in the predicted area of the experiment container. This unexpected result would be the subject of continued research by scientists at Hamilton Standard and other institutions.

Aaron Gillette, whose experiment was sponsored by the Martin Marietta Corporation, wanted to find out how zero gravity affected the growth of sponges. Preliminary results showed that the sponge cells were able to grow in space, although there seemed to be some peculiarities in their growth patterns. Further analysis of Aaron's sponges is being conducted at Martin Marietta and at Western Carolina University.

Scott Thomas's experiment on convection— circulation in heated liquids—confused the experts. The experiment, sponsored by Thiokol Corporation,

One of the three SSIP experiments on STS-5 was Aaron Gillette's study of the growth of sponges.

Left: Scott Thomas displays the complicated equipment for his SSIP experiment on convection in zero gravity. Below: Scott and R. Gilbert Moore of Thiokol Corporation in the shuttle mock-up at Johnson Space Center.

was conducted in space by astronaut Joe Allen, but post-flight analysis could not determine whether convection had actually occurred in zero gravity. NASA finally decided to repeat Scott's experiment on a later shuttle mission.

One of the most important things that all the SSIP experiments have had in common is that every one has led to further investigation and more experiments. In this respect, each is an example of valid scientific inquiry, contributing not only to the student's education but also to the growth of scientific knowledge in general.

The continued expansion of the Shuttle Student Involvement Project will give even more young scientists an opportunity to participate in this exciting endeavor. In 1983, NASA and the National Science Teachers Association increased the number of national finalists to 20 and began to schedule the winners' experiments on future shuttle flights. Alan Ladwig, SSIP program director, expects greater participation each year as the program becomes better known among science students and teachers. Plans are underway to expand the SSIP program to include high school students in Canada, and a similiar student program is being developed in Europe.

In a press conference following STS-5, astronaut Joe Allen talked about the SSIP program and the student participants. He said, "I think they should let their imaginations be their guide. The more imagination, the better experiment it will be.... I'll wager someday [a] student will be there in orbit, working on his or her experiment."

Alan Ladwig, SSIP program director for NASA (left), and Helen Marie Hoffmann, SSIP program manager for the National Science Teachers Association (right), talk with Richard Cavoli, a finalist in the second SSIP competition, held in 1982.

Todd Nelson did not have the opportunity to conduct his own experiment in space as future SSIP winners may be able to do, but he played an important role as the first student whose experiment flew on the shuttle. Just as STS-3 was the Pathfinder mission in the space shuttle program, Todd's "Insect in Flight Motion Study" was a scientific pathfinder in the Shuttle Student Involvement Project. Todd's experiment paved the way and set the standards for the other student experiments that came after it.

At 2:32 A.M. on August 30, 1983, the space shuttle *Challenger* made a spectacular predawn liftoff from Kennedy Space Center. On board this eighth shuttle mission was Wendy Angelo's SSIP experiment, which was designed to test the use of biofeedback training in space.

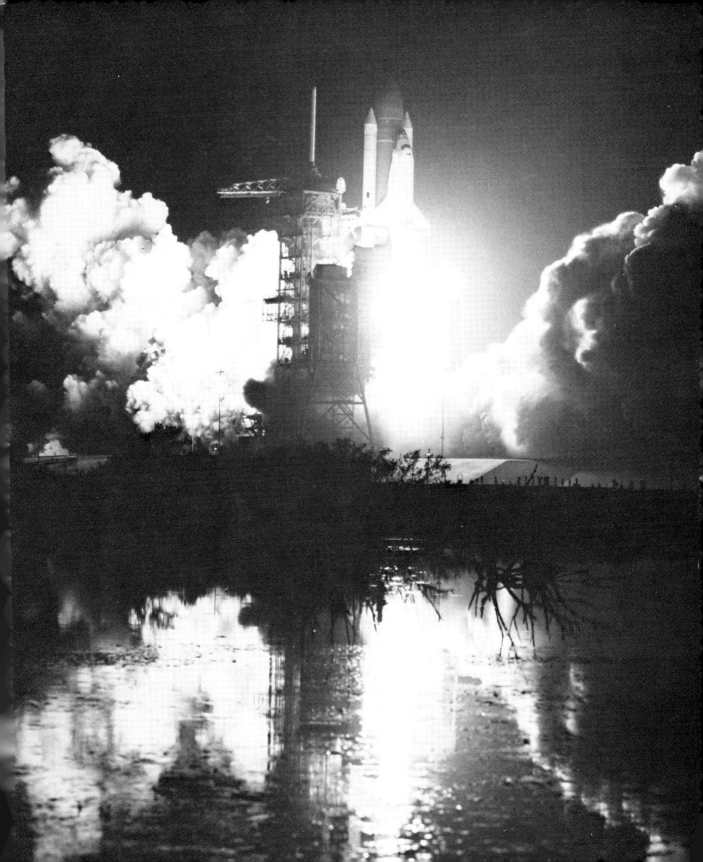

AUTHOR'S ACKNOWLEDGMENTS

I would like to express my appreciation to the following individuals who contributed in many ways to Todd's experiment and to this book: Alan Ladwig and John Jackson, National Aeronautics and Space Administration; Dr. Helen Marie Hoffman and Dorothy Culbert, National Science Teachers Association; Leonard David, National Space Institute; Dr. Norman Leppla, United States Department of Agriculture; Dr. David Pimentel, Cornell University; Gerald W. Adams, Dr. J. Robert Peterson, William J. Steinbicker, Patsy Brown, Susan Vekich, Alex Allen, Thomas Jacobus, Kathi Poppitz, Honeywell, Inc.; Robert Roberts, Southland High School; and, of course, Todd Nelson and his parents, Dale and Sherry. I would also like to give special thanks to my wife, Sally, for her editorial advice, thoughtful support, and patience. Finally, I would like to thank my editor, Sylvia A. Johnson, for lending her particular talents of writing, editing, and organization to this book.

PHOTO ACKNOWLEDGMENTS
The photographs and drawings in this book are reproduced through the courtesy of: pp. 2, 20, 79 (bottom), 91, 104, Minneapolis *Tribune* (Mike Zerby); pp. 8, 10, 12, 14, 16, 31 (right), 36, 46, 68, 74, 76, 78, 85, 86, 87, 88, 90, 92, 93, 110, 113, 114, 116, 117, National Aeronautics and Space Administration; pp. 17, 75, 80, 94 (bottom), 95, Tom Jacobus; pp. 18, 31 (left), 33, 34, 84, National Science Teachers Association; pp. 21, 79 (top), Robert Roberts; pp. 22, 23, Dale Nelson; p. 24, *Odyssey* Magazine (Phil Heckman); pp. 26, 30, 45, 50, 51 (top), 55, 61, 89, 102, 105, Todd Nelson; pp. 28, 38, 39, 40, 41, 44, 56, 62, 63, 83 (bottom), 94 (top), Honeywell, Inc. (Ray Roberts); p. 43, William J. Steinbicker; p. 47, J. Robert Peterson; pp. 48, 51 (bottom), 52, 54, 64, 120, Patsy Brown; pp. 53, 57, 58, 59, 60, 82, 83 (top), 107, 109, Robert R. Moulton; pp. 66, 67, Phil Steinberg; p. 69, David Pimentel; pp. 70, 103 (right), United States Department of Agriculture; p. 72, New York State College of Agriculture and Life Sciences, Cornell University; p. 81, Gerald W. Adams; p. 96 (top), *The Florida Times-Union*; p. 96 (bottom), Rochester *Post Bulletin*; p. 97, Linda Gilles and Sharon Loeschen; pp. 98, 106, 108, Delbert E. Philpott; p. 103 (left), Norman Leppla; p. 112, McDonnell Douglas Corporation. Cover photographs courtesy of National Aeronautics and Space Administration (color) and Minneapolis *Tribune* (black and white).

Author Robert R. Moulton (left) with Todd and Honeywell team members Jerry Adams and Bob Peterson

ROBERT R. MOULTON is public relations manager for the Aerospace and Defense Group of Honeywell, Inc., the corporate sponsor of Todd Nelson's SSIP experiment. He served as Honeywell coordinator of the project, and FIRST TO FLY is based on his unique first-hand knowledge of the people and events involved. Moulton is also the author of a paper on Todd's experiment presented at the International Astronautical Federation Congress held in Paris in September 1982. His other written works include many articles published in business and technical journals.